CW01500695

Contents

KEY TO TRANSLITERATION AND PRONUNCIATION OF
SANSKRIT LETTERS

Sanskrit is a highly phonetic language and hence accuracy in articulation of the letters is important. For those unfamiliar with the *Devanāgari* script, the international transliteration is a guide to the proper pronunciation of Sanskrit letters.

अ	a	(b*u*t)	ट	*ṭa*	(*t*rue)*3
आ	ā	(f*a*ther)	ठ	*ṭha*	(an*th*ill)*3
इ	i	(*i*t)	ड	*ḍa*	(*d*rum)*3
ई	ī	(b*ea*t)	ढ	*ḍha*	(go*dh*ead)*3
उ	u	(f*u*ll)	ण	*ṇa*	(u*nd*er)*3
ऊ	ū	(p*oo*l)	त	ta	(pa*th*)*4
ऋ	r̥	(*rh*ythm)	थ	tha	(*th*under)*4
ॠ	r̥̄	(ma*ri*ne)	द	da	(*th*at)*4
ऌ	l̥	(reve*lry*)	ध	dha	(brea*the*)*4
ए	e	(pl*ay*)	न	na	(*n*ut)*4
ऐ	ai	(*ai*sle)	प	pa	(*p*ut) 5
ओ	o	(g*o*)	फ	pha	(loo*ph*ole)*5
औ	au	(lo*u*d)	ब	ba	(*b*in) 5
क	ka	(see*k*) 1	भ	bha	(a*bh*or)*5
ख	kha	(bloc*kh*ead)*1	म	ma	(*m*uch) 5
ग	ga	(*g*et) 1	य	ya	(lo*y*al)
घ	gha	(lo*g h*ut)*1	र	ra	(*r*ed)
ङ	ṅa	(si*ng*) 1	ल	la	(*l*uck)
च	ca	(*ch*unk) 2	व	va	(*v*ase)
छ	cha	(cat*ch h*im)*2	श	śa	(*s*ure)
ज	ja	(*j*ump) 2	ष	ṣa	(*sh*un)
झ	jha	(he*dg*ehog)*2	स	sa	(*s*o)
ञ	ña	(bu*nch*) 2	ह	ha	(*h*um)

•	ṁ	*anusvāra*	(nasalisation of preceding vowel)
:	ḥ	*visarga*	(aspiration of preceding vowel)
*			No exact English equivalents for these letters

1.	Guttural	–	Pronounced from throat
2.	Palatal	–	Pronounced from palate
3.	Lingual	–	Pronounced from cerebrum
4.	Dental	–	Pronounced from teeth
5.	Labial	–	Pronounced from lips

The 5th letter of each of the above class – called nasals – are also pronounced nasally.

MOMENTS WITH ONESELF SERIES: 9

FREEDOM

SWAMI DAYANANDA SARASWATI

ARSHA VIDYA

ARSHA VIDYA
RESEARCH AND PUBLICATION TRUST
CHENNAI

Published by :
Arsha Vidya
Research and Publication Trust
32 / 4 ' Sri Nidhi ' Apts III Floor
Sir Desika Road Mylapore
Chennai 600 004 INDIA
Tel   : 044 2499 7023
Telefax: 2499 7131
Email   : avrandpc@gmail.com

ISBN : 978 - 81 - 904203 - 9 - 6

Revised Edition : August 2007   Copies : 2000
1st Reprint   : May   2009   Copies : 2000

Design :
Suchi Ebrahim

Printed by :
Sudarsan Graphics
27, Neelakanta Mehta Street
T. Nagar, Chennai 600 017
Email : info@sudarsan.com

No proof is necessary to establish the existence of 'I'. I am self-evident, while everything else is evident to the self. Being self-evident, I do not depend on anything else for my existence. In any given experience I become the invariable factor. Whether I see, hear, taste, touch or smell the presence of 'I' is not cancelled. I am always present; I hear the sound, see the form, enjoy the touch, taste or smell. When a given object goes away from my vision, still the presence of 'I' remains. It continues to be present to objectify something else. Thus, in every form of knowledge, I am always there without undergoing any change.

Now, consider two objects such as a table and chair. The existence of one does not depend upon the existence of the other. If the chair is destroyed, the table can exist. Similarly, if the table is removed, the chair is present. The two are co-existent, each independent of the other. However, there are things in the world that are mutually dependent. There is no husband without his wife and no wife without her husband. The presence of one accounts for the presence of the other. Between the world and myself, however, the relationship is neither one of mutual independence nor mutual dependence. I exist independent of any object, whereas the existence of the object is dependant on me, the invariable self.

EVERY OBJECT IS REDUCIBLE TO SOMETHING ELSE

In my hand I have a styrofoam cup. If I ask you what is in my hand, you say it is a cup. If I say it is styrofoam, am I right or wrong? I am right; but then so are you when you say it is a cup. We now have two distinct words referring to the same object. We cannot say that both words are wrong, or that one is wrong while the other is right. If both are right, are they equally right? If two words refer equally to the same object, then the words are synonyms. You never say, "Bring me a glass of water with some aqua in it," because aqua and water are synonyms, referring to the same thing. If the words 'styrofoam' and 'cup' are also synonyms, then wherever there is a cup, there should be styrofoam and wherever there is styrofoam, it should be a cup. The truth is, however, different. The cup need not be styrofoam, and the styrofoam need not be a cup. Each has its own object to convey. But here there is only one object, styrofoam cup. Therefore, I must necessarily know that although both words are right, they are not equally right. One must be more right than the other. Which is more right? One person says that the word 'cup' is more right. I say that 'styrofoam' is more right. Suppose, I tear the styrofoam cup into two pieces, where is your cup now?"

Previously I said there was styrofoam; now also I can say there is styrofoam. My styrofoam stays, whereas your cup no longer holds water! The cup is definitely gone now. Has it walked away from the styrofoam? No, because there is never an independent object called cup. There is only a particular form for which you have a name, called cup. You can never think of a cup or any other object without a substance. The cup is dependent for its existence on that substance, and here the substance is styrofoam. The styrofoam, on the other hand, is not dependent on the cup. With reference to the cup, it is self-existent. However, even the styrofoam is not a final substance, because it is reducible to some other substance. The final substance is that which is not further reducible, not dependent on any other substance for its existence. The final substance, therefore, can never be an object because any object has a form that is reducible to something else.

VEDANTA IS ALL ABOUT TWO FACTS

What cannot be an object can only be the subject, the invariable 'I' which is self-existent, never dependent on another. The 'I' is, thus, *satya*, the substantive and everything else depends upon *satya* for its existence. The dependent is not *satya* but neither it is non-existent or false; the non-existent cup cannot hold water. In a given form it is called a cup and it does hold water. This dependent reality that is neither non-existent, or even false, is *mithyā*.

In Vedanta there are only two facts to understand— *satya* and *mithyā*. Definition of *mithyā* is that which draws its existence from the presence of something else. Therefore, any object is *mithyā*. For example, the object we call 'car' is made up of hundreds of things put together. If you take the steel away, where is the car? Though the car is not self-existent, it is neither an illusion nor a delusion; it is *mithyā*. You know it by a means of knowledge and it is useful.

When an object exists, 'I' awareness is; and when the object is destroyed, 'I' awareness continues to be. Therefore, 'I' awareness, is independent of any given object. Similarly, when time and space are resolved, as in deep sleep, still 'I' awareness is. If awareness were not present in sleep, on waking, you could never say that you slept. Therefore, 'I' awareness is free from both time and space. 'I' awareness is not just the historical I; it is neither made up of memory nor a personality. All these depend on 'I' awareness; they too are *mithyā* while 'I' awareness alone, free from all attributes, is *satya*.

If 'I' alone is *satya* and everything else is *mithyā*, then nothing can compare itself to 'I'. In fact, one *satya* plus *mithyā* does not equal to two because *mithyā* is not something separate from *satya*. Styrofoam plus the cup is still styrofoam. Suppose, a jeweller buys one ton of gold and makes one million ornaments from the gold. He makes different sizes and shapes of chains, bangles, rings and so on. Are there two different things here? No. One ton gold plus one million ornaments is equal to one. That is why Vedanta says that the truth is non-dual.

Vedanta is not monism. Mono means one, and one is always available for fractioning, for becoming many. There is one universe but many galaxies; one galaxy but many systems, one system but many planets, one planet but many continents, one continent but many countries, one country but many states, one state but many counties, one county but many houses, one house but many bricks, one brick but many atoms, one atom but many particles. What do you mean by one? In fact, there is no second thing.

One plus *mithyā* is still one; this is what we say is non-dual. *Satya* is one, and that is you. Add the whole world, both known and unknown, and it is still one. This knowledge makes a great difference in one's life, as we shall now see.

IF THE STYROFOAM CUP HAS A HUMAN MIND!

Imagine the cup having a human mind. It is now self-conscious. With a self-conscious mind, it will have some opinion about itself, and all the complexes that we have. The ways of the mind would be the same, the cup saying, "I am a small cup, but the other cup is a big one. They only keep cold water in me even though it is winter, while that other fellow has sugar and sits there so nicely. Look at the china cup. They go on polishing it, treasuring it, and keeping it in the cupboard all the time. But nobody cares about me. I am dispensable, I am not going to last, I shall die one day, soon."

The cup becomes depressed and seeks a solution to its problems. One person tells the cup that it has to go on a special diet. In the morning it should eat sprouts and leaves, in the evening brown rice and lentils. Another person tells the cup to stand on its head daily, so that more blood will flow to the head. This is certainly beneficial, but it will also mean that if the cup thought wrongly before, now it will think more wrongly! The cup only becomes an upside-down cup. Still it will be a cup; it does not become something else. Another person tells the cup that it has deep impressions inside which the cup must remove. Still another says that the cup must dive deep into itself to discover its true nature, styrofoam.

IF THE CUP WERE TO BE TAUGHT

If I were to teach the cup, however, I would not say any of these things. I would simply tell the cup, "You are not a cup; in fact you are styrofoam." Though the cup is styrofoam, styrofoam is not a cup. That is self-knowledge. The cup need not be afraid of being a cup; it should know that if it breaks, the 'I' is not broken. The conclusion that "I am a mortal" will not be there if the cup knows that the 'I' is bio-non-degradable styrofoam. Now there are a million styrofoam cups. If I am a cup, I am different from all of them, and they are different from me. But if I am styrofoam, then all of them are 'I'; I am not any of them. All cups exist in me because I am *satya*, the basis of all of them.

RECOGNITION OF THE TRUTH

All that is required then is the simple recognition that, 'I', self-evident awareness, am *satya*; everything else is *mithyā*. While the body is 'I', while the senses and thoughts enjoy 'I' who is awareness, the 'I' is not any of them. While the knower, knowledge and object known all enjoy awareness, 'I' awareness itself is not dependent on any of them. They come to light because of me; they depend on me for their existence. Therefore, the world cannot really stand apart from me. When there is no division between the world and me, what is the possibility of something limiting me? Neither a time limit nor a spatial limit nor an object limit is possible, because everything is 'I', from the 'I' standpoint. Suppose, the cup shifts the 'I', with the knowledge, back to the cup; then it is an enlightened cup. As a cup it has its limitations in that it can hold only so many ounces. But it is now free enough to enjoy the limitations of the cup.

Similarly, if the world is *mithyā*, it cannot really inflict any harm on you. The world cannot make you unhappy. You need not remove any thought to become happy or to discover the true self, just as you need not remove the wave to discover water. Our problem is that we think 'I' is thought, which is incorrect. We erroneously identify with the thought and become sad and unhappy. The solution is, recognising that while the thought is 'I' the 'I' is not the thought. Even while thinking, I am free, just as the actor remains free while playing the role of the beggar.

Once this is recognised, then the world cannot cause a problem for you. Vedanta does not remove any of the limitations centred on the individual's body, mind and senses; it only makes one understand that the individual is already free in spite of them.

THE 'I' IS DISTINCT FROM EVERYTHING ELSE

In any experience there is both subject, the experiencer, and object, the experienced. Sensory experience such as seeing, hearing, smelling, tasting or touching, involves a division between the subject and the object. All these experiences reveal to us a person who is different from the world being experienced. As a seer, hearer, taster, thinker, you are the subject, the experiencer, and the objects of your experience are separate from you.

Everyone else around you is also an object of your experience; none is you, the experiencer. Moreover, every person in the world can say the same thing. Thus, everybody else is other than you because everyone else is an object of your experience. This only confirms that you are distinct as a person separate from everything else.

'Everything else' is the whole universe, and you are separate from that everything else, in the sense, that you are only a tiny speck in this universe of many things. Seeing yourself in this vast universe, you say, "I am distinct from all these countless things." You never look upon yourself as one of the countless things in the universe; you look upon yourself as one who is distinct from the countless things. All things that you see are things that 'you' see. They are 'seen' and you are the 'seer'. The seen, all the things that exist, is separate from you and you are separate from them. Thus, your experience, involving the divisions of seer-seen, knower-known reveals an isolated being, small and distinct from everything else, and this is confirmed with every experience, be it pleasant or unpleasant.

IN DEEP SLEEP THERE IS FREEDOM FROM ISOLATION

In contrast to this experience of duality, another form of experience exists that is free from isolation—the experience of deep sleep. In deep sleep you do not see anything, you do not hear anything, you do not think anything; therefore, the division of thinker-thought, and of seer-seen does not exist. Even though sleep involves no division, it is a valid experience because you relate to that sleep as the one who experienced it. On waking you recount the experience of sleep and say, "I slept well," similar to the statement "I ate." In both these statements you are recalling a past event; the present narrator, you, is the same as the experiencer of the prior event. If you were not there in sleep and are only in the here-and-now, you could never relate the fact of your having slept. Thus, it is the same 'I' that is there as the deep sleeper, as the dreamer, and upon waking up that same 'I' is the waker. In sleep the experience is not one of isolation. it means you experience yourself as a person free from isolation on a daily basis, whenever you are in deep sleep.

FREEDOM FROM ISOLATION IN A MOMEMNT OF JOY

This freedom from isolation also occurs in the waking state, for there are moments when one does not seem isolated from anything. When you undergo a happy experience, you have a moment of joy. In this moment of joy, you see yourself not as an isolated being but as a happy, free being. You find yourself related to a world that does not isolate, a world that makes you feel whole, as the stars do sometimes, as a sunrise or sunset does sometimes, as the hearing of music or the laughter of a baby does sometimes. A division, a subject-object relationship, is involved here, the subject, you, as well as the stars, the sunrise, the sunset. Yet in spite of this relationship, you find that the objects do not isolate you. You seem to be one with them because you have no sense of smallness. In fact, the object seems to make you happy. On the other hand, were you to feel separate from them and see yourself as an isolated being, you could never enjoy the stars, much less laugh with the baby.

Two types of contradictory experience

There are, then, two types of experience. One, the experience of isolation wherein one has the notion "I am small" and, two, the experience of non-isolation, the experience of the whole in spite of one's perception of various objects.

Gaining experience is not freedom from isolation

Once there is the experience of non-isolation, then one can never stand smallness and isolation. One seeks non-isolation and completeness time and again, and one tries to avoid conflicts in relationships and to live in harmony with one's surroundings. Whenever a conflict arises we experience isolation that goes against the complete being that we know experientially. We try to solve this isolated feeling by doing many things. However, the more one does, the more one finds oneself isolated. One may, by chance, pick up a moment of fullness; however it is not a rule that gaining this experience or that, one will become full, free from isolation.

GETTING RID OF A THING IS ALSO NOT FREEDOM FROM ISOLATION

Conversely, ridding myself of a thing will not guarantee fullness, because the very object I throw out, someone else may pick up as a windfall! When I see the fact that there is no rule for being full, I have initially gained what is called *viveka*, discrimination. I now understand that seeing something need not bring isolation and that gaining something will not free me from isolation.

THE HUMAN STRUGGLE STEMS FROM THE TWO CONTRARY EXPERIENCES

Further, I am able to appreciate the fact that the struggle of the human being stems from these two contrary experiences, one, the experience of non-isolation, and two, the experience of isolation. One can see why a human being has such difficulty in accepting himself or herself as a small, isolated being; for the notion of smallness is contradicted by an experience of the opposite nature.

VEDANTA ADDRESSES THE PROBLEM OF ISOLATION

In tackling these two contradictory experiences, one must examine which experience is true to one's nature. Is smallness or fullness the truth about oneself? Does one struggle to feel small or is one's quest all about feeling complete? In a happy situation one strives to cling to that fullness. One does not struggle to get rid of one's happiness in order to feel isolated. On the contrary, there is an effort to maintain that happy experience in which one feels no desire for change. It is, therefore, clear that the experience with which one is 'at home' is the one wherein there is freedom from want. That experience should be the reality about oneself, natural to oneself; but whether it is natural or not, it is the only experience for which one struggles. One may not even think about it being the truth, an untruth, or a half-truth, but having known it very well experientially, one wants that one thing alone, fullness.

These contradictory experiences, thus, comprise the frame of reference within which you communicate on a daily basis. If these contradictory experiences were eliminated, no one would struggle in life. The struggle you undergo is not merely for attaining food, shelter, and clothing, since the acquisition of these still leaves a human being, wanting. What you need and strive for is to overcome your sense of isolation so that you can feel in harmony with your set-up. Indeed, whatever be the immediate set-up, that set-up constitutes your universe. If you cannot strike harmony with the people around you, you will never feel one with the universe. The entire universe, in fact, is but the few things in your immediate surroundings. A person, or even a flower is all you require to constitute the universe. When you look at a flower, that is the universe. That is the entire world with which you have to strike harmony. Whenever you do strike harmony, having got rid of isolation, you are at home with yourself. In harmony, you see yourself as a whole person.

Vedanta addresses this problem of isolation and the wish to be free from isolation. It cites your experiences and tells you that what is desirable and sought after, and in which you feel at home is yourself. That self is not created. Neither achievement nor loss creates that self. Wholeness is your nature.

ISOLATION IS DUE TO THE WRONG NOTION OF THE SELF

If I am the whole, which I experience occasionally, what is it that separates me from the whole?

When I sleep, I do not feel isolated; when I am awake, I feel isolated, although not all the time. Occasionally, I feel that I am happy and full. What creates this isolation that is not in keeping with my nature? I cannot say that it is the world or the sense organs, or the mind, because whenever I am happy, when I see a world with which I am happy, the mind still is. The sense organs and the world still are. None of these things isolate me.

What isolates me can only be a wrong notion about myself, and consequently about the world. This thinking is characterised by the conviction that there is a struggle in life, a struggle based on the conclusion that I am an isolated being. That conclusion does not go away in spite of a contradictory experience. Even though occasionally I experience myself to be free from isolation, still that experience does not destroy the conclusion that I am an isolated, small being. The experience only fans my desire to be free from isolation because it becomes the norm for me, and I cannot settle for anything less. That happy experience becomes more a basis for continuing my struggle to seek harmonious experiences than a cause for the affirmation of myself as a full being.

This conclusion that one is separate from the universe that traps and overwhelms one is not removed by experience because experience does not pass as knowledge. One is supposed to learn from experience, and what one learns from experience is called knowledge. Experience provides the basis for immediate knowledge. If one wants to have immediate knowledge of some object, that knowledge can take place only when one experiences the object. Mere experience, however, is not knowledge; one needs to know that very experience.

THE GAIN OF SELF-KNOWLEDGE IS FREEDOM FROM ISOLATION

Since everyone experiences the self as a whole, complete being, why should I feel small and isolated? It is because although the experience comes and goes, I do not have knowledge of my true nature. If I know that I am full, how can I conclude against that knowledge and take myself to be just the opposite? I cannot, just as I do not dismiss the sun as non-existent after sunset. Experientially the sun is gone, but I still say that the sun is. In my mind I know that the sun is not gone, even though it cannot be seen. Similarly, the conclusion that I am a small, isolated being goes against the truth of my nature and results in problems. This conclusion does not go unless I learn otherwise, by analysing both types of experience and unless I know, for good, that my nature is wholeness.

When this knowledge is gained, what happens? Once you recognise you are the whole, you are the whole whether you see the creation or do not see the creation, whether you do something in the world or do not do anything. The whole does not acquire a dent by your doing something, or by your not doing something. This knowledge is called liberation, freedom; the freedom that everyone loves, wants and struggles for.

No one is interested in bondage and isolation. You cannot say that one person is a seeker whereas another person is not. However, a special word, *mumukṣu*, is used for the one who knows himself or herself to be a seeker of this freedom. Until you discover you want freedom, you are not called a *mumukṣu* even though freedom is what you seek. Everyone seeks, but not everyone knows that he or she is seeking. This is because not everyone sees liberation as an end to the problem of isolation.

Vedanta gives you the knowledge of your true nature. Gaining this knowledge one finds that one is free from all forms of limitation and isolation. Full and complete in oneself, one strikes harmony with the entire universe.

HUMAN LIFE IS A PRIVILEGE

It is a great privilege to be a human being because we can say so! I do not know what a monkey would feel when I say that I am a privileged person. But the poor monkey cannot make the statement: "I am privileged to be a monkey." Our scriptures praise the human life: *jantūnām narajanma durlabham,* meaning that among all living beings, the birth as a human being is scarce indeed.

What really distinguishes a human being from all other living beings on this planet? A peculiar physical body cannot be the basis for such a privilege. In fact, every animal has its own features. But, in the human being alone there is a great capacity and that is the capacity to make choices. I can make a choice. I can talk to you with a commitment to communicate the topic I want to. This choice is given to me.

CHOICE GOVERNS HUMAN LIFE

If there is anything in which I do not have a choice, it is in exercising this faculty of choice. Even when I do not deliberately make a choice, I am choosing the default option. The kind of clothes I wear, the kind of food I eat, and the attitudes with which I eat are all open to choice.

Exercising choice is a very important thing and necessarily implies that you should know what to choose. You cannot afford to be ignorant of certain things. The Government expects that you know everything about the laws that they have enacted because in a court of law ignorance is no excuse. So too in life, you cannot afford to be ignorant with reference to living.

GOAL OF LIFE IS LIVING

Somebody asked me the other day, "Swamiji, what is the goal of life?" The man is 55 years old, and he is asking me this question! Obviously, he has not found a satisfying answer to this basic question. What can be the goal of life? Some would say it is going to heaven. If this is so, why should I come here to go to heaven? Is it a detour? Another person says the goal of life is death. Upon death I am going to be absent which I was already before birth! Why was I born then? Therefore, neither death nor going to heaven can be the goal of my life. In fact, the goal of life is just to live.

To be alive is one thing, but to live your life is quite another. A person in a state of coma is alive, and with all the support system that we have these days the person can be kept alive for years. But that is not living.

LIVING IS RELATING TO THE WORLD

To live you have to relate to the world. Even an animal has to relate to the world. One who refuses to relate to the world need not be blessed with senses and other faculties. In this relating, how objective you are or how well you are able to exercise the faculty of choice, determines how far you have come towards achieving your goal. To accomplish different things, you must relate to the world intelligently, exercising the freedom of choice.

Often we are more mechanical than free. If there is a motor set to revolve so many times per minute, that motor does not have any freedom of choice to revolve in any other manner. It will perform as it is programmed; that is mechanical. If the clouds gather and the atmosphere is conducive, the rains happen. There is no choice on the part of the clouds. This too is mechanical. Under certain conditions, certain things happen. For our purpose of understanding, we shall call the choiceless happenings as reactions, in contrast to the actions based on free choice. If we are to achieve the goal of living, we must learn to make conscious, free choices and avoid being mechanical.

REACTION IS MECHANICAL

Suppose, I request you all to clap; well, some of you may clap, others may not clap, and still others may clap differently. You are free in your action. You may clap once, twice, three, or even five times. The freedom is literally in your hands. When you decide to clap, you are conscious of what you are doing; in other words, you are alive.

Now, I ask you to be angry just for a minute. Go on. What happened? Are all of us angels? (Laughter). You can never get angry simply because someone has asked you to. You may say, "No swamiji, I do get angry, but I do not know when I will be angry." Anger happens. It does not require your permission. Anger is a reaction. Similarly, jealousy, sadness, and sorrow are all reactions. If you permit yourself to be angry, you will be pretending, and your child will know that. When you are really angry, your child will run far away from you. Anger is something that happens, and in anger what happens is more reactions.

A reaction is something that happens without your being conscious of it. You are what your psychology is, more so than your intellect. You may have certain cognitive skills, and you may have understood difficult intellectual concepts, but those alone do not constitute the human life. You can be successful and learned and still be a miserable person in relating to the world. You can be an ordinary person in a village without any credentials and certificates and still be a successful person in life, if you know how to relate to the world.

Everyone has to become a swami

Therefore, our scriptures, which are highly pragmatic, want you first to be a Swami, a master. You have to grow into a Swami. You have to cut down your mechanical-ness for which you have to understand how to relate to the world intelligently. Unless you are conscious of what you are doing, your mind cannot serve you and your memory cannot guide you. Anything that happens without your being conscious of it is a reaction.

You are an actor when you are free in your action. You can choose your action and not submit to the pressure of your environment. You may even be obliged to conform to what is happening around you, but then that is your choice. It is not because of pressure you choose to do what others do. If it is your choice, you will be able to change, alter and even give it up also. If others do and pressurise you to do it, then necessarily you are going to face problems in life that do not belong to you at all. Therefore, whenever you choose, you have to be careful to see what you will gain in the bargain. Will you surrender your choice? Will you lose your freedom?

TO RELATE IS TO RESPOND CONSCIOUSLY

One needs to be extra cautious while relating to other human beings because they too enjoy the privilege of exercising choice. It is easy to relate to a dog or an elephant because one can study the pattern of their behaviour. They are already programmed. But you cannot completely know a human being; he or she is unpredictable. How can you relate to a human being, who also exercises his or her own choices?

If we use our choice wrongly, it may be out of ignorance. However, ignorance is not a problem for relating with a person, really. We are all born ignorant. One thing we need not work for is ignorance. To shed ignorance, of course is a privilege that we have. A donkey does not have that privilege. It has no freedom whether to do, not to do, or do it differently. If it feels like kicking, it will kick; it has no choice.

The animals have reactions, responses that are naturally programmed, and are more often predictable than not. If not predictable, it is only a failure or inadequacy of our understanding of these animals.

On the other hand, a human being is not totally programmed. Therefore, you have to respond consciously. You can kick, you need not kick, or you can choose to do it differently; after having lifted your leg, you can place it differently. Similarly, when you use words that hurt another person, you abuse the words. More often than not you are not deliberate. And that means you regret what you said and then say, "I did not mean it at all." You do things without meaning to do them. What kind of respect can the other person have for you? Even you will not have any self-respect for yourself. All that you have—your education, culture, status, prestige, and everything about the person—is unavailable when you act mechanically and when you fail to exercise your choice.

CHOICE IN ACTION IS THE PRIVILEGE

There is freedom in action only when you choose to act. You have no freedom in action when you allow things to happen to yourself. This is something that every human being should know. As long as you are conscious of your action, you can learn from it. You can correct your mistake. However, if it is a reaction, you do not learn anything from it. In fact you have to learn to avoid it, because you would do the same thing and say: "I did not mean it at all." That is a pitiable life! We have to live on this planet together. You can expect me to be conscious of what I say, and I can also expect you to be conscious of what you do. If you are inimical to me, at least I can know that you are inimical without becoming an enemy myself.

What we call *dharma* consisting of universal values stems from conscious living. You know very well what you do not want others do to you. You want the people, indeed the whole world, to behave properly towards you. Even a thief with a knife in his hands expects the woman of the house to tell the truth, "Where are the keys?" That means you want the world to behave in a certain manner that is conducive to you. Insofar as others' behaviour is concerned, you have no doubt at all. Everybody should be caring, loving and truthful. Nobody should be deceptive and angry with you. You are very clear about this.

Unfortunately, the world also expects you to behave in the same manner. If you do not behave as expected by the world, it may very well be by your conscious choice. This capacity to choose makes you a very privileged living being. It becomes a blessing for you when you use it, and a curse if you misuse or abuse it. Therefore, you have to examine, in your daily life, whether you are employing your conscious choice in talking and in interacting with people. If you are having difficulty in choosing, you can always consult someone.

The *Taittrīyopaniṣad* says:[1]

"If you have to make a choice and if you get confused as to what is right and wrong, go to those people in the contemporary society who are given to a life of *dharma*, who are dispassionate and, therefore, have a capacity to be objective. Go to them, talk to them and follow their advice till you gain an understanding and maturity to make proper choices."

This is one of the most profound sentences in our scriptures. There cannot be a better advice than this one.

---

[1] *Yāni anavadyāni karmāṇi tāni sevitavyāni no itarāṇi;*
atha yadi te karmavicikitsā vā vṛttavicikitsā vā syat
ye tatra brāhmaṇāḥ saṃmarśinaḥ
yuktāḥ āyuktāḥ alūkṣāḥ dharmakāmā syuḥ
yatha te tatra varteran tatha tatra vartethāḥ (1.11)

LIFE IS A CHALLENGE

Some people say that one has to go through the experience to understand. Nobody goes through the experience of getting electrocuted to understand what electrocution is! And so, until you understand, follow what the wise say. If they do not understand your situation, talk to them so that they do.

This is not at all a sermon from a Swami. This is just saying that the privilege of being a human being on this planet is to live a responsible life. Life is full of challenges, and without challenges life is nothing.

Let us look at this situation. A great philanthropist spent millions to build a stadium and dedicated it to the city. The inauguration was with a soccer game. He invited his uncle from his village to come and watch the game. The uncle had never seen a soccer game. While watching he became sad and said to the nephew, "I do not understand you. You have spent a fortune on this stadium and yet you are so miserly that you have provided only one ball for the 22 players. Should you not give 21 more balls? All the 22 players are chasing that one ball. See how they are fighting for it!"

If 21 more balls are given, there will be no soccer game. It is having one ball that makes the game a challenge. If everyone had a ball, then there is no game. The real challenge in life is not merely in a classroom or a lab; these are challenges all right. However, in the lab of life, the challenge is to be conscious; you have to choose what you want to do.

If you understand the beauty and the privilege of living a conscious life even for one moment, well, your entire life is made glorious in spite of the limitations. This is freedom in your action.

You are free to the extent you grant freedom to others, to the people you are connected with. For instance, when you buy a ticket, say, to go to Mumbai, even though you buy just one ticket, you know there are twenty others who travel with you requiring no ticket! The people who bother you are always with you. It is because you carry them in your head.

Lord Kṛṣṇa in the *Bhagavad Gītā* says,[2] "Keeping the external objects external ..." Should He say that? "Allowing the sun to be in the sky..." should He say that? It is already in the sky. Would you say, "Allowing the sun to be in the sky, allowing the stars to appear in the night, allowing the fire to be hot, allowing the water to find its own level." You are not allowing anything here. Why does the Lord say, "Allowing external objects to be in the external world?" It is because you carry them in your head.

A Vedic mandate says, "No one should drink alcohol." But nowhere does it say, "Do not drink molten iron." It is because no one drinks molten iron.

---

[2] *sparśānkṛtvā bahir bāhyān...* (5.27)

A mandate is there only when there is a necessity for it. It is because we carry people in our heads, our scriptures tell us: "Keep them outside."

It is easier said than done. You are hurt; you want the people's behaviour to change. You want them to talk to you a little softly; you want them to be a little more understanding, a little more giving, a little different. There is nothing wrong in this because you have to live with these people; and unless they change, you are not going to be happy.

You want them all to understand you better, to be more liberal, and more sympathetic towards you. But then they are not so. People want you to be different. Everyone thinks something is wrong with the others. When we really want people to be different and when we want certain changes to happen in our lives, there is clearly an external world involved.

You are connected to the external world, and this you cannot get rid of. This external world has a capacity to enter into you, stay with you and weigh you down. How can you take this weight off?

Is there anyone who is outside his or her own psychological make-up? Can you be outside the laws that govern the physical world?

If you are standing and you do not levitate and fly away, it is because of certain laws. Similarly, can anybody be free from the laws that govern biology, physiology, and so on? They are all one vast network of laws. There is no exception from them. A person's behaviour at a particular time and place is explainable because of these laws.

Like any other law, psychological laws are not created by human beings. Similarly, the laws that govern knowledge and error, the laws of epistemology and so on, are also not created by human beings. There are laws that govern our memory and our recollection. We look upon this vast network of laws as the Lord. Whether we accept God, these laws are definitely there. In the scriptures it is said that the person from whom all laws emanate is the Lord, Īśvara, and what has come from him is not separate from him.

If this is understood, even in a small measure, it can give you some space to allow people to be what they are. The more you understand a person to be what he or she is, the more you can help the person change if you think that such a change will be for the better, for you and the other person. You can help only when you keep the person outside of your mind.

When you keep the person inside, he or she troubles you so much that whenever you talk to that person you can never be reasonable, and that person becomes a bore, a red rag for you. You will, more often than not, be unreasonable in anger. If at all you wish to change someone, you have to be a resonable person. To be reasonable is to be compassionate and understanding. To understand a person you have to see where does the person come from and the more you see this, the more you are able to appreciate and understand the person. This is not an ordinary thing. It is something that makes the difference between the person who can enjoy the world and oneself and the one who carries the load in his or her head unnecessarily.

People ouside cannot get into you if you have proper emotional or cognitive immunity. You can protect yourself from this world and the world is no longer a source of danger. The world is like you inasmuch as you affect the world and world affects you. You do not allow yourself to be affected by the world by keeping the world where it is.

You cannot change the background of a person. If that person wants to change, he or she can change, and you can, perhaps, help. For instance, if you know of a dangerous, contagious disease and how it spreads, you will know how to equip yourself, immunize yourself and protect yourself. In the same way, one great protection is to understand that people cannot be changed and each one's behaviour is according to his or her own nature. The more you understand this aspect of people, the more you will learn how to deal with them. If you wish a person to change, and you are sure that the wish cannot be fulfilled, then convert the wish into a prayer. You pray and with that understanding, half your mental load is gone.

Prayer is the only action that has got the total free will to back it up. In every other form of action or choice, the free will is stifled. It is afflicted by one's own pressures of agenda and by the circumstances of the situation. Therefore, in all decisions in life, the free will is not totally fee. However, in prayer there is total free will. You need not pray at all. You are free to hit your head against the wall or go on a buying spree, but you choose to pray.

Prayer comes from the free self. It is a complete manifestation of inner freedom. Or I would say it is the manifestation of your total freedom. If the free will has any freedom, it is total, and it is available. When the free will is afflicted, it is more a reaction than action.

Whereas, prayer is total action and action produces results. After all, your resources, time, and energy are limited. What you can do is not to throw up your arms but bring your palms together and pray. That is freedom.

Prayer gives you the inner freedom. The more you understand people, the more you are free. The more you give them freedom to be what they are and draw boundaries to protect yourself, the more freedom you enjoy. At the same time you do not want to be entirely indifferent. They are outside your boundary and continue to be there. You have love for them. You can care for them from where you are. There is no concern and anxiety. This is called trust in the Lord. In your prayer include them and you will feel lighter inside. Vedanta will walk into you when you have that kind of lightness inside.

Oṁ Tat Sat

BOOKS BY SWAMI DAYANANDA SARASWATI

Public Talk Series :

1. Living Intelligently
2. Need for Cognitive Change
3. Discovering Love
4. Successful Living
5. The Value of Values
6. Vedic View and Way of Life

Upaniṣad Series :

7. Muṇḍakopaniṣad
8. Kenopaniṣad

Moments with Oneself Series :

9. Freedom from Helplessness
10. Living versus Getting On
11. Insights
12. Action and Reaction
13. The Fundamental Problem
14. Problem is You, Solution is You
15. Purpose of Prayer
16. Vedanta 24x7
17. Freedom
18. Crisis Management
19. Surrender and Freedom
20. The Need for Personal Reorganisation
21. Freedom in Relationship
22. Stress-free Living

Text Translation Series :

23. Śrīmad Bhagavad Gītā
    (Text with roman transliteration and English translation)

Stotra Series :

24. Dipārādhanā

25. Prayer Guide
    (With explanations of several Mantras,
    Stotras, Kirtans and Religious Festivals)

Bhagavad Gītā Series :

26. Bhagavad Gītā Home Study Program
    Vol 1-4 (Hardbound)

27. Bhagavad Gītā Home Study Program
    Vol 1-4 (Softbound)

Meditation Series :

28. Morning Meditation-prayers

Essays :

29. Do all Religions have the same goal?

30. Conversion is Violence

31. Gurupūrṇimā

32. Dānam

33. Japa

34. Can We?

35. **Teaching Tradition of Advaita Vedanta**

Exploring Vedanta Series : (*vākyavicāra*)

36. śraddhā bhakti dhyāna yogād avaihi
    ātmānaṁ ced vijānīyāt

BOOKS BY SMT. SHEELA BALAJI

37. Salutations to Rudra
    (based on the exposition of Śrī Rudram by
    Swami Dayananda Saraswati)

38. Without a Second

Also available at :

ARSHA VIDYA RESEARCH
AND PUBLICATION TRUST
32/4 Sir Desika Road
Mylapore Chennai 600 004
Telefax : 044 - 2499 7131
Email   : avrandpc@gmail.com

ARSHA VIDYA GURUKULAM
Anaikatti P.O.
Coimbatore 641 108
Ph   : 0422 - 2657001
Fax   : 0422 - 2657002
Email : office@arshavidya.in

ARSHA VIDYA GURUKULAM
P.O.Box 1059. Pennsylvania
PA 18353, USA. .
Ph   : 001-570-992-2339
Email : avp@epix.net

SWAMI DAYANANDA ASHRAM
Purani Jhadi, P.B. No. 30
Rishikesh, Uttaranchal 249 201
Telefax : 0135-2430769
Email : ashrambookstore@yahoo.com

AND IN ALL THE LEADING BOOK STORES, INDIA